DISCOVER ANCIENT CIVILIZATIONS

DISCOVER ANCIENT GREECE

Kim A. O'Connell

Enslow Publishers, Inc.
40 Industrial Road
Box 398
Berkeley Heights, NJ 07922
USA

http://www.enslow.com

Ancient Greece at the time of the legendary Trojan War, c. 1200 B.C.

Copyright © 2014 by Enslow Publishers, Inc.
All rights reserved.

No part of this book may be reproduced by any means without the written permission of the publisher.

This book previously published as *Ancient Greece* in 2004.

Library of Congress Cataloging-in-Publication Data:
O'Connell, Kim A.
  Discover Ancient Greece / Kim A. O'Connell.
     p. cm. — (Discover ancient civilizations)
  Includes bibliographical references and index.
  Summary: "Learn about the art and cultural contributions, family life, religions and people of ancient Greece"—Provided by publisher.
  ISBN 978-0-7660-4196-7
  1. Greece—Civilization—To 146 B.C.—Juvenile literature. I. Title.
  DF77.O26 2014
  938—dc23
                           2012011572

Future editions:
Paperback ISBN 978-1-4644-0335-4   Single-User PDF ISBN 978-1-4644-1187-2
ePUB ISBN 978-1-4645-1187-5   Multi-User PDF ISBN 978-0-7660-5816-3

Printed in the United States of America

112013 Lake Book Manufacturing, Inc., Melrose Park, IL

10 9 8 7 6 5 4 3 2 1

To Our Readers: We have done our best to make sure all Internet Addresses in this book were active and appropriate when we went to press. However, the author and the publisher have no control over and assume no liability for the material available on those Internet sites or on other Web sites they may link to. Any comments or suggestions can be sent by e-mail to comments@enslow.com or to the address on the back cover.

Every effort has been made to locate all copyright holders of material used in this book. If any errors or omissions have occurred, corrections will be made in future editions of this book.

Enslow Publishers, Inc., is committed to printing our books on recycled paper. The paper in every book contains 10% to 30% post-consumer waste (PCW). The cover board on the outside of each book contains 100% PCW. Our goal is to do our part to help young people and the environment too!

Photo Credits:
© Clipart.com/© 2012 Photos.com, a division of Getty Images. All rights reserved., pp. 2, 21, 42, 45, 49, 52-53, 55, 74(inset), 86, 90; ©2012 Photos.com, a division of Getty Images. All rights reserved., pp. 14, 18-19, 35, 37 (Athena and Zeus), 61; ©Corel Corporation: pp. 37 (Hermes and Poseidon), 59, 66-67, 69, 81; ©Enslow Publishers, Inc.: pp. 37 (Aphrodite, Atlas, Gaia, Hades, Persephone, and Prometheus), 95; Associated Press/AP/Julie Jacobson, Staff , p. 81; Feodor Vasilevich Korolevsky/© 2011 Photos.com, a division of Getty Images. All rights reserved., p. 87; Muharrem Zengin/© 2011 Photos.com, a division of Getty Images. All rights reserved., pp. 92-93; Natalia Pavlova/© 2012 Photos.com, a division of Getty Images. All rights reserved., pp. 10-11; PANAGIOTIS KARAPANAGIOTIS/© 2011 Photos.com, a division of Getty Images. All rights reserved., pp. 74-75; Shutterstock, pp. 2-3, 30-31, 37(Demeter), 70, 73, 78-79; The White House, pp. 46-47

Front Cover: iStockphoto/© 2013 Thinkstock. All rights reserved.(background); ©Corel Corporation(inset)

Table of CONTENTS

CHAPTER 1
The Land and Early History.... 7

CHAPTER 2
Life of the People..................... 24

CHAPTER 3
Ancient Greek Government.... 40

CHAPTER 4
The City-State and Wars.......... 51

CHAPTER 5
Great Legacy of Arts
and Culture 64

CHAPTER 6
Alexander the Great 85

Timeline...................................... 97

Glossary 99

Chapter Notes 101

Further Reading and
Internet Addresses 102

Index 103

Chapter 1

The LAND and EARLY HISTORY

Discover Ancient Greece

The landscape of ancient Greece made it highly unlikely that a great civilization would develop there. There were too many mountains, no major rivers where water and rich soil allowed people to grow enough food, and no vast open plains where a civilization could flourish.

Covering the southern part of the Balkan Peninsula, ancient Greece was hilly and rugged. About three quarters of its territory was mountainous, and only about a quarter of the land along the coast and small valleys was suitable for farming.

Ancient Greece was made up of three distinct geographical regions. Northern Greece included portions of ancient Macedonia and low-lying coastal plains. Central Greece was capped by the highest point in Greece, Mount Olympus, which was believed to be the home of the gods, and Athens, the capital of modern-day Greece. Southern Greece included the

The Land and Early History

Peloponnese, a peninsula that thrust into the Mediterranean Sea. It housed another great ancient city—Sparta. Southern Greece was connected to central Greece by a narrow isthmus at Corinth. Ancient Greece also boasted numerous islands sprinkled throughout the Aegean Sea, an arm of the Mediterranean Sea between Greece and Turkey. Two of the largest islands, Crete and Rhodes, were mostly mountainous.

The climate of ancient Greece was semi-arid, with long, hot summers and short, rainy winters. The weather varied greatly from region to region, ranging from long periods of drought to heavy, flood-causing rainstorms. The lack of adequate rainfall along the hilly landscape meant the ancient Greeks could not produce enough food to support themselves.

The Aegean and Mediterranean seas also dramatically impacted the lives of the ancient Greeks. Most of the region was near

The Treasury of Atreus was built during the Mycenaean period. Kings were usually buried in these chambers. Because of the many beautiful objects buried with them, these graves were known as "Treasuries."

Discover Ancient Greece

the seas. It was easier for the Greeks to travel by sea than over the rugged, mountainous landscape. They also traveled the seas to settle on the islands off the mainland where they established colonies along trade routes to secure the goods they needed.

Early Settlers

The territory of ancient Greece was populated as early as the Stone Age, when humans survived by hunting and gathering food, using tools made of stone, wood, and bone.

One of the first major civilizations that developed in this region was the Minoan. It developed about 3000 B.C., on Crete, an island in the Mediterranean Sea. The Minoans ruled that part of the world until about 1450 B.C. However, the Minoans were not Greek.

The first ancient Greek civilization began around 2000 B.C. during the Bronze Age, when wandering tribes migrated south into

The Land and Early History

the Balkan Peninsula. This civilization, the Mycenaean, was named after the city of Mycenae in the Peloponnese. The Mycenaeans were warriors and sailors who took control of the region, including the island of Crete, where the non-Greek Minoans had created a wealthy civilization. The late Mycenaean period, from 1400 B.C. to 1100 B.C., was marked by cultural advances and the beginnings of classic Greek mythology.

The Mycenaean kingdoms were regional states, each ruled by powerful kings and warlords from fortified palaces, called citadels. The mighty walls of the citadels were ten feet thick and surrounded by the fields and villages of farmers and craftsmen—all controlled by the king. At its height, the Mycenaean civilization was powerful and wealthy. This civilization was long considered to be an age of warrior heroes, but it would only last about three hundred years.

Discover Ancient Greece

A mask of beaten gold was found placed over the face of a dead Mycenaean king.

« 14 »

The Land and Early History

At one time, people dismissed these stories of early Greek history as myths. However, in the late nineteenth century, a series of archaeological digs revealed great Mycenaean palaces surrounded by massive walls, archives written on thousands of clay tablets (in a script called Linear B, most of which were accounting records listing materials and goods,), elaborate wall hangings, and elaborate tombs with skeletons covered with gold and jewels. Other excavations uncovered evidence that the Trojan War—one of Greece's most beloved myths—was actually based on a real war.

The Trojan War

Archaeologists believe that the Trojan War was based on a conflict fought around 1200 B.C. between invading Greeks of Mycenae and the people of Troy, a prosperous city on the east coast of the Aegean Sea in what is today Turkey. Although the exact history may never be known, most Greek understanding of the Trojan War comes from Homer, one of the greatest Greek poets. He described the Trojan War in two epic poems attributed to him, *The Iliad* and *The Odyssey*.

According to mythology, the Trojan War began when Paris, the Trojan prince, kidnapped Helen, wife of Menelaus, the king of Sparta. When the Trojans refused to return Helen, Menelaus persuaded his brother King Agamemnon of Mycenae to lead an army against Troy. The Greeks sent a fleet of a thousand ships to Troy to recapture Helen. The war waged on for nearly a decade, until the Greeks destroyed Troy after deceiving its citizens by hiding soldiers in the Trojan horse.

Dark Age and Renaissance

By 1200 B.C., the cities of the Mycenaean civilization were destroyed and the palaces of the great kings were burned. Historians

The Land and Early History

are not sure why this civilization declined so rapidly. The Dorians from northern Greece invaded around 1100 B.C. and occupied these cities that had been weakened by war. Thucydides, an Athenian historian, described the end of the Mycenaean civilization in this way: "The return of the Greeks from Troy after such a long time caused many changes; in general, there was civil strife in the cities, and exiles from these founded other cities.... And eighty years after the War, the Dorians occupied the Peloponnesus with the Sons of Heracles."[1] Heracles, or Hercules, was a mythical Greek hero known for his feats of strength.

This threw ancient Greece into a period of decline known as the Dark Age that lasted about four hundred years, until 800 B.C. The advanced communities of the Mycenaeans disintegrated after the Dorian assault, and Greeks lived in small, isolated

The lion gate, part of the citadel walls of Mycenae, was built during the third stage of the fortress's construction in 1200 B.C. The gate protected the palace and administration buildings as well as homes. The huge slab over the opening is 15 feet long and 7 feet thick.

villages, growing just enough food for their own families. The art of writing disappeared, and most record keeping ceased. After producing a rich variety of cultural artifacts in previous periods, the Greece of the Dark Age left behind little evidence of its culture. Most historians believe this was a period of migration that dispersed Greek citizens to settle new colonies. The Greeks established colonies west of the Greek mainland in what is today Italy. They also formed colonies in the eastern Aegean. These colonies were called Ionia. These Greek colonists were separated from the political and religious communities of the mainland.

By 900 B.C., Greek civilization began to recover. Pottery was produced more often and featured more complex designs. After a period in which subjects were limited to animals and geometric figures, Greek art began to feature human activity once again,

The Land and Early History

The great wooden horse loomed at the gates of Troy after the Greek besiegers had apparently withdrawn. The Trojans, curious, brought it into their city. At night, the Greeks emerged from the wooden horse and captured the city. Homer tells this story in *The Illiad*.

....

possible evidence of a renaissance, or rebirth, in Greek culture and society. The most significant cultural contribution of the Greek renaissance occurred around 800 B.C. when the Phoenician alphabet was adopted to write the Greek language. The Greek alphabet consisted of twenty-four letters and is still used in Greece. The term "alphabet" comes from the first two Greek letters, *alpha* and *beta*. The alphabet spread to all parts of the Greek world and helped unite its people culturally.

The Rise of the Greek City State

Toward the end of the Dark Age of Greece, the population increased and small villages grew into cities. Greek communities called city-states began to develop. A city-state, called a *polis*, consisted of a city or town and its surrounding farmland and villages. It was often a lowland central area surrounded by protective hills. Each city-state was independent of the others and each had its own history, economy, culture, and type of government. The citizens of each polis would often quarrel among themselves and seldom acted together except when they were threatened by invasion.

The Land and Early History

By around 700 B.C., there were more than a thousand city-states in the Aegean area. Ancient Greece was not a single, unified country. Even though the ancient Greeks spoke a common language, they had no single leader, unlike the civilizations in ancient Egypt and Persia. Two of the most advanced city-states were Athens, the urban center of Attica, and Sparta, in the southwestern Peloponnese.

Chapter 2

LIFE of the PEOPLE

Life of the People

Although Greece is known as the birthplace of democracy, for much of its history ancient Greece had an extremely divided society—with a distinct upper class and a lower class. The upper class was made up of aristocrats, wealthy land owners who controlled most of the city-states. The lower class was made up of peasants and slaves. Peasants were commoners who lived under the rule of the aristocrats. The peasants were technically free, but they were often indebted to their landlords. Slaves were sometimes owned by the government and placed in supportive roles such as police officers or secretaries. Private slaves would either did farmwork or household chores.

The aristocrats were known as *hoi agathoi,* or "the good," while the peasants were called *hoi kakoi,* or "the bad." Another term for this class was *hoi polloi,* which is still used today to describe the common people of a society.

Discover Ancient Greece

Although ancient Greece was a class-oriented society, wealthy and poor citizens lived in similar style homes. Family homes were simple wood, mud brick, or stone buildings, with a series of rooms arranged around a courtyard. These structures included an *andron*, which was a men's dining room that was decorated or had a marble floor. The buildings were often painted a bright white to reflect the hot Mediterranean sun.

The arrangement of private houses offers an example of early urban planning. In most Greek city-states, the city center included a dense concentration of private homes, which were connected by narrow streets and broken up by garden plots. All the private and public buildings were arranged around an open space, called an agora, where community meetings were held and goods were offered for sale.

Life of the People

Farming and Clothing

Although only a small portion of Greece could be farmed, the Greeks did successfully cultivate the "Mediterranean triad" of crops—grain, grapes, and olives. From these, Greeks made bread, wine, and olive

A Greek house had a courtyard with an altar in the middle of it.

oil, which were the staples of their diet and are still popular in Greek cuisine today. The ancient Greeks also ate peas, beans, fruits, and nuts in abundance. High-protein foods such as cheese, meat, and fish were also eaten, but in smaller quantities, almost as a relish for the meal. The Greeks did not like butter and drank little milk, preferring water or wine instead. Honey and spices were used to sweeten or season foods.

Greek farmers also kept flocks of sheep, goats, and pigs. Oxen and mules were valued for plowing and pulling loads, and cattle were raised for their meat and hides. Only the members of the upper class kept horses, which were used for riding and pulling chariots.

The clothing of the ancient Greeks was simple but well suited to the climate and the surroundings. Made by the women of the household, as well as any female slaves, most clothes were rectangular in shape and

Life of the People

required little sewing. Men wore simple tunics of linen or wool, while women wore long garments called *peplos*, which were gathered at the waist and pinned at the shoulders.

Trade

Because the seas were close to almost all parts of ancient Greece, trade became an important part of life for the Greeks. The Greeks built cargo ships to export any surplus products, such as olive oil, wine, and grain. They traded among the Greek islands and with colonies that were overseas as well as with foreign lands.

Family Life

Modern understanding of Greek family life comes primarily from Athens, which preserved family rituals in vase painting, tomb sculptures, and dramatic stories. In Greek society, before citizens could become members of the polis, they first

Discover Ancient Greece

This stonework from an ancient Greek column shows a woman (center) with a man to the left of her. The woman is dressed in a rectangle of woolen fabric wrapped around the torso and pinned at the shoulder. The man is dressed in a simple tunic, a linen cloth draped over both shoulders and drawn in at the waist.

« 30 »

Life of the People

« 31 »

had to be accepted into a family group, known as the *oikos*. Fathers determined the fitness of the child upon birth and decided whether the child would be kept or abandoned to die. If the child was healthy and accepted into the family, the happy news was announced with the hanging of olive wreaths or tufts of wool on the front door. If children were abandoned, they would sometimes be raised and sold as slaves. Once accepted into a family, a boy would also be approved for membership in his father's *phratry*, or brotherhood, which was a clan of relatives that protected each other.

    Men usually married when they were thirty years old, while women usually were married at age fifteen. Women came to the marriage with a dowry, a gift of money or property, for her new husband. During the wedding, the father of the bride would say to the groom, "I give you my daughter to sow for the purpose of producing legitimate

Life of the People

children," to which the groom would agree by answering, "I take her."[1] Greeks often married members of their own family. Household duties were divided: outside work for the men, including plowing and planting, and inside work for the women, including sewing and cooking.

Education

Greece's two rival city-states, Athens and Sparta, had very different ideas about how youth should be educated. In ancient Athens, education was for the wealthy aristocrats. The purpose of education was to train children in the arts and literature. Girls were not allowed to attend school, but they were taught at home to read and write. After some home schooling, boys were often sent to a small neighborhood school where they memorized famous passages written by Homer or taught to play a musical instrument called the lyre.

Discover Ancient Greece

Other subjects may have included reading, writing, math, and playing the flute. In their teens, males went to a high school and then to a military school, graduating around age twenty. The upper class could afford to send their children to private tutors.

In Sparta, education centered almost entirely on military training. At the age of seven, Spartan boys were sent to military school. There they lived in barracks and trained to be warriors. To toughen them up, boys were forced to go barefoot, sleep on rough mats, and were encouraged to steal. At the end of their teen years, males had to pass a test of their fitness and military skills to become soldiers. If they failed, they were banished to the middle class. Spartan girls were sent to military schools where they were taught wrestling, gymnastics, and combat skills. If their women were strong, Spartans believed, they would produce strong babies—the soldiers of the future.

Life of the People

Greek Red Figure Vessel Of Students At The Athenian School. Instruments of instruction, mostly musical ones like a lyre, hang on the walls. One instructor is correcting the exercise of a boy who stands before him. Another is showing how to play the flute. The seated figures with staffs are "pedagogues."

Gods and Religion

Ancient Greeks believed that many gods and goddesses directed their everyday lives. In Greek society, citizens worshiped their gods at traditional altars, often making ritual sacrifices of animals. The earliest Greek religions were actually a mix of elements from Asia and Egypt. Eventually, through various works of literature, the wide range of Greek gods and goddesses began to be clearly organized. Myths were written about their origins and activities. In Homer's *Iliad*, the gods were portrayed as a tight-knit family group, residing on Mount Olympus. The remarkable aspect of the ancient Greek religion was that the gods were given human traits and displayed human emotions and weaknesses. These gods and goddesses resembled humans, but they were immortal and had special powers. Each god or goddess represented a

Gods and Goddesses

The ancient Greeks worshiped many gods and goddesses. Each god or goddess oversaw one or more aspects of Greek life.

Aphrodite—Goddess of love and beauty.

Athena—Goddess of warfare, wisdom, and arts and crafts.

Atlas—Part of the special group of gods called the Titans, Greeks believed Atlas held up the sky.

Demeter—Goddess of farming.

Gaia—Goddess of the Earth.

Hades—God of the dead and the underworld.

Hermes—Messenger of the gods.

Persephone—A goddess whom the Greeks used to explain the seasons.

Poseidon—God of the sea.

Prometheus—Part of the special group of gods called the Titans, Greeks believed he gave fire to humans.

Zeus—Ruler of the gods. God of sky and weather.

Discover Ancient Greece

different human trait or force of nature. Citizens appealed to these gods for help in their lives, and city-states often adopted a god or goddess as its representative.

Throughout the ancient world, there were shrines, called oracles, where ancient Greeks could seek advice from the gods. They believed that Delphi was the center of the world and many of them made pilgrimages to seek advice from the god Apollo, often identified with the sun, who lived there. People consulted a priestess who would go into a trance and pass messages to and from the gods. These messages were often difficult to interpret.

Zeus, god of the heavens and defender of justice in the universe, was thought to be the leader of the Olympians. According to myth, Zeus had many wives and companions, but the most famous was Hera, the most beautiful Olympian. Zeus also had many powerful children. Among them

Life of the People

were Aphrodite, the goddess of love; Ares, the god of war; and Persephone, goddess of the seasons. In one of the most famous myths, Zeus' son Heracles was forced to perform twelve tasks, or labors, including wrestling a lion and killing a multi-headed snake called the Hydra.

Chapter 3

ANCIENT GREEK GOVERNMENT

Ancient Greek Government

The ancient Greeks introduced the idea of a democratic form of government, one in which ordinary citizens participated directly in decision making. The word *democracy*, or rule of the people, comes from two Greek words: *demos*, which means "people," and *kratos*, which means "strength" or "rule." In a democracy the people hold the most power. Democracy was just one form of government practiced by the ancient Greeks.

The Polis

The centerpiece of ancient Greek government until 338 B.C. was the polis or city-state. City-states were independent and self-governing. In ancient Greece, this meant that city governments could range from absolute monarchies—led by a single ruler—to democracies ruled by the vote of the people.

Discover Ancient Greece

Map of the Greek city-states

Ancient Greek Government

Greek city-state governments usually consisted of an assembly and a council. In democracies, assemblies were the primary political power, composed of citizens. In oligarchies where a few powerful people ruled, the council had the final say, representing the small group of leaders—usually a family unit—that held power. Although city-states sometimes combined into larger religious or military organizations, most were constantly in danger of attack by other city-states. For example, Greece's two most powerful cities—Athens and Sparta—had very different styles of government. Their intense rivalry led to the devastating Peloponnesian War.

At first, small city-states required few officers. Athens had several dozen officeholders at the end of the sixth century. A century later, that number had increased to about seven hundred political officers. Political offices were not organized into hierarchies, although the chief officer was usually called the *archon,* which means "leader," or *prytanis,* which means "president."

Athenian Democracy

The city of Athens is known as the birthplace of democracy, which began around 507 B.C. when Cleisthenes, an Athenian statesman, came to power. Democracy would develop gradually over the next two hundred years. Cleisthenes, an aristocrat, proposed a constitution in which all male adult citizens automatically became members of the assembly. At that time, there were about thirty thousand members. On important matters the entire assembly met to decide the issues. The assembly elected a council of five hundred men who directed the government's daily business.

For the first time, ordinary citizens, who were not aristocrats or rich, could participate. But the Greeks had a limited definition of

Ancient Greek Government

Male citizens were able to speak their minds freely in government councils.

citizen. Only men, eighteen years of age or older, of Greek origin were considered citizens and therefore allowed to vote; women, children, and slaves were not. In addition, a person's social status factored heavily in his participation. In Athenian politics, the wealthier and more socially connected the candidate, the more likely he could gain office. Citizens over the age of thirty could serve as jurors on the people's court.

President Barack Obama gives his State of the Union address in 2012. Many modern governments have been influenced by the democratic system that developed in Athens in the fifth century B.C. Democracy in ancient Greece, however, was different from what it is today—a sizeable chunk of Greek society including women, foreigners, and slaves, did not have the vote.

Another reform permitted the assembly to banish citizens from political activity. This process was called *ostracism*. Each man took an *ostrakon*, or pottery shard, and wrote on it the name of a citizen whom he wished to exile. If one person received more than six thousand votes against him, he was banished from Athens and not allowed to return for ten years. Some of the city's greatest heroes were ostracized because the Athenians grew jealous of their power and influence.

The fundamentals of democracy instituted by the ancient Greeks have endured and are still practiced in the United States and other democratic societies in the world. These fundamentals include the decision of a majority vote, the right to a trial by jury, and the ability to question or even recall political leaders. Celebrating democracy, Euripides wrote that, in Athens, "Our city is not subject to one man. No, it is free, for here the people rule."[1]

Ancient Greek Government

A naval commander and statesman, Themistocles arranged for the evacuation of Athens before the invasion by Persian forces. Later, he was ostracized from Athens.

The Spartan Mix

Sparta's government was a mix of monarchy, democracy, and oligarchy. Spartans favored keeping political power in the hands of a monarch or a council of elders. However, Sparta eventually saw the value in creating a system of checks and balances so that the government could not easily take a swift, radical action. To achieve this, Sparta created a dual-king government. Not only did the two kings cooperate on political issues, but they also protected Sparta from ever being without a ruler. The council included the two kings and a group of twenty-eight elders who prepared material

Discover Ancient Greece

for the assembly. Sparta also established an assembly of citizens—all men over the age of thirty—who could accept or reject proposals, but were not allowed to discuss them. Unlike the city-state of Athens, there were no people's courts in Sparta.

Chapter 4

The CITY-STATE and WARS

Discover Ancient Greece

Although its name implies something old or outdated, the Archaic Age of ancient Greece (700 B.C.–500 B.C.) produced some of Greek society's most influential cultural contributions. It was during this time that the Greek city-state form of government took hold. This was also a time of colonization. The lack of adequate farmland forced the Greeks of the Archaic Age to explore the Mediterranean from one end to the other, establishing hundreds of colonies along the way.

Art, architecture, literature, and philosophy all flourished. Two dominant artistic techniques—called "black figure" and "red figure"—emerged, in which silhouettes are

The City-State and Wars

The 2,500-year old bas-relief at Behistun is a World Heritage Site near Kermanshah in Iran. It shows Darius holding a bow, as a sign of kingship, and treading on the chest of a figure who lies on his back before him. It also shows 10 smaller figures representing defeated enemies.

painted on pottery in one color or another with details cut into them. These innovations greatly increased international trade and extended the Greek influence.

However, with the strengthening of Greek city-states came increasing conflicts among them. On the Peloponnese, the three city-states of Sparta, Argos, and Corinth began to fight over territory. Despite this, the Archaic Age spurred a greater sense of cultural unity among Greek city-states, which would be strengthened in the coming wars against Persia.

The Persian Wars

Between 500 B.C. and 449 B.C., Greek city-states fought four major battles against the powerful Persian Empire, which included all of western Asia and Egypt. Under the tyrannical rule of King Darius I, Persia had hoped to invade and add the Greek city-states to its vast domain. Many of the city-states united together to ward off the invaders.

The City-State and Wars

The Greeks were facing invasion by Darius of Persia, whose warships landed in the Bay of Marathon. Despite being heavily outnumbered the Greeks surrounded the enemy troops and drove them back to the sea, losing only 192 men, while 6,000 Persians perished.

In 490 B.C., Persian forces planned an attack on Athens. Both armies met on the coastal plain of Marathon, twenty-six miles northeast of Athens. Even though the Athenians were outnumbered two to one, they defeated the Persians in a decisive battle, slaughtering more than six thousand Persians. According to legend, a messenger ran nonstop the twenty-six miles from Marathon back to Athens to announce the victory. After delivering his message, he collapsed and died from exhaustion. Today, in honor of that legendary run, the distance of the race known as a marathon is 26.2 miles long.

Ten years after Marathon, the Persians launched another massive invasion. It was led by Darius' son, King Xerxes I. The king ordered two bridges made of ships to be built and tied side by side so the Persian armies could cross over the Hellespont, a narrow strait in northwestern Turkey

The City-State and Wars

connecting the Aegean Sea to the Sea of Marmara. The Persian Army, with more than three hundred thousand soldiers, outnumbered the Greek Army of only ten thousand soldiers. Led by King Leonidas of Sparta, the Greek Army went north to defend the narrow mountain pass at Thermopylae, a strategic location that served as the gateway to southern Greece. Here is where the Persians would cross to invade Athens and Sparta. A traitor told Xerxes about a mountain pass that would position the Persians behind the Greeks. When Leonidas realized he was trapped, he dismissed all the soldiers except three hundred men from his Spartan city-state. The Spartans, bound by a pledge to fight, did not retreat. Instead, they attacked the Persians. Every single Spartan soldier, including Leonidas, was killed. This is known as one of the most heroic battles in world history. The Persians continued on and conquered Athens, much of which they burned down.

By this time, Athens had developed the greatest naval force in ancient Greece under the direction of Themistocles. He ordered a fleet of two hundred *triremes*, warships that were quick and easy to maneuver. Shortly after Thermopylae, Themistocles lured the Persian fleet into a narrow channel off the island of Salamis. The triremes fought and devastated the Persian Navy. This was the turning point in the wars with Persia. In the final battle that took place at Plataea, the well-trained Spartan forces defeated what remained of the Persian land forces.

After these victories, Greece became united when Athens formed the Delian League, in which about two hundred city-states agreed to cooperate with each other in common defense against the Persians. As a result of the wars, Athens became the

The City-State and Wars

This depiction of Spartan charioteer riding into battle appears on the Vix Crater, a large vessel found in France and believed to be Spartan, c. 520 B.C.

most powerful city-state and Sparta became the second most powerful. The victory over the Persians was a turning point in the ancient Greek history. It saved Greece from foreign rule. Historians still debate how different the world would be if Xerxes had conquered Greece and it had become part of the Persian Empire.

An Ancient Rivalry

The two very different societies of Athens and Sparta sparked one of the key rivalries of ancient Greece.

Athens was named for Athena, the Greek goddess of wisdom and war. Athena was a fitting symbol because ancient Athens saw both outstanding cultural, political, and intellectual achievements and long periods of warfare and strife. Athenian leaders encouraged development of the arts and literature and fostered an open, democratic society.

The City-State and Wars

This statue shows the goddess Athena holding Zeus' head. Athena, the daughter of Zeus and Metis, was a guardian of Athens, where the Parthenon was erected as her temple.

Discover Ancient Greece

Sparta was a rigid society whose ruling class enforced discipline, simplicity, and obedience. Spartan citizens trained for war from an early age and remained soldiers all their lives. Today, the word *spartan* is still used to describe something that is disciplined, restrained, or basic.

Athens had the strongest naval power; Sparta had the strongest and most disciplined land power. Athens headed the Delian League. Suspicious of Athens' growing power, Sparta formed the Peloponnesian League. These two rivals struggled to dominate the ancient Greek world.

The Peloponnesian War

A war between Athens and Sparta began in 431 B.C. Early in the war, it appeared that the Athenian fleet had the upper hand, winning several victories. However, about 430 B.C., a plague killed nearly one quarter of Athens' population, including its leader,

The City-State and Wars

Pericles. Sparta conquered several Athenian cities, including a decisive victory at Amphipolis in 422 B.C. Eager to punish its old enemy, Persia helped Sparta to create a fleet to fight the Athenian Navy. This first fleet was destroyed, but another Spartan fleet won a key naval battle. Despite their losses, the Athenians repeatedly declined to make peace. Finally, under the command of Lysander, the Spartan fleet destroyed the Athenian Navy in 405 B.C., forcing Athens to surrender the following year. The war changed Sparta from a distrustful, isolated city-state into a world power.

Historians believe that Sparta's greed and self-serving power contributed to both its own decline and the weakening of traditional Greek society as a whole. As the Greek orator Isocrates wrote, "[I]n some citizens, power was the cause of injustice, depravity, disrespect for the laws and greed for riches."[1]

Chapter 5

GREAT LEGACY of ARTS and CULTURE

Great Legacy of Arts and Culture

Throughout the modern world, one can see the influence of ancient Greece, whether through replicas of ancient Greek temples, the continuing tradition of the Olympic Games, or in poetry and the arts. Ancient Greece can even be heard in our language: Many English words and phrases are derived from Greek roots.

Many, but not all, great achievements came during the Classic Age (500 B.C.– 400 B.C.) and particularly so during the Golden Age of Greece under Pericles, the leader of Athens. The Golden Age was brief, lasting only thirty years. It began after the Persian Wars, when Athens had to rebuild, and ended when Sparta defeated Athens in the Peloponnesian War. During this era, Athens rose to economic and political supremacy to become the most powerful city in the ancient world. It was the center of a trade network for goods

The Parthenon was built in Athens between 447 and 432 B.C. to replace two other temples on the Acropolis honoring the goddess Athena. The structure represents the city-state's growing domination of Greece as well as the power and influence of its builder, the statesman Pericles.

from all over the world. The Athenians produced great art, architecture, literature, and philosophies.

Pericles was a statesman who had a great vision for Athens. He wanted Athens to become a city that would lead an empire. Pericles believed that the ideal citizen should participate in his city's government. He felt that politics was the business of every citizen. During his rule, Pericles spent large sums of money on massive reconstruction projects, especially public buildings that everyone could use: gymnasia, theaters, law courts, and public dockyards.

Art and Architecture

Greek cities were often planned around a tall hill called an acropolis, which was reserved for grand temples to the gods. Greek temple architecture has influenced builders and designers through modern times. Greek temples featured a rectangular structure with

Great Legacy of Arts and Culture

This relief was part of a frieze that ran around the Parthenon. It depicts ancient Greek horsemen riding through Athens to the Acropolis in a religious procession The frieze wrapped around the entire building and was 524 feet long.

Ionic columns with their distinctive scrolls can be seen on the Jefferson Memorial in Washington, D.C.

Great Legacy of Arts and Culture

a porch on one or both ends that was flanked with vertical columns. One famous example of this style is the Parthenon, a marble temple in Athens that Pericles had built and dedicated to Athena.

There were three styles of columns, distinguished by the top part of the columns called the capitals. These capitals were called Doric, Ionic, and Corinthian. The capital of the Doric column is plain; the Ionic has scrolls; and the Corinthian has carved stone leaves. Examples of these styles can be seen in many public buildings today. In Washington, D.C., alone, Doric columns can be found on the Lincoln Memorial, Ionic columns on the Jefferson Memorial, and Corinthian columns on the U.S. Supreme Court building.

Pediments, or gables, of temples were decorated with sculptures of gods and goddesses, carved to look like perfectly formed human beings. Those on the

Parthenon show the birth of Athena and a contest between Athena and Poseidon, the Greek god of the seas.

Literature and Philosophy

Ancient Greece also produced two of the most studied works of literature in world history—Homer's *Iliad* and *Odyssey*—that serve as a model for most epic poetry produced ever since. Epic poems are long stories about national heroes that were written in verse and usually sung or recited before an audience. Sappho was a Greek poet who wrote about friendship, love, and nature.

    The Greeks also created the idea of plays. They wrote and performed many comedies, tragedies, and satires. The three best-known dramatists were Aeschylus, Sophocles, and Euripides. The early Greek dramas involved dialogue between a lead singer and a Greek chorus. In the plays of

Great Legacy of Arts and Culture

This statue, The Hermes of Praxiteles, though so mutilated, remains one of the world's masterpieces.

« 73 »

An artist's interpretation of what a Greek drama might have looked like.

In sacred sites like Epidaurus, people gathered to see dramas in honor of the gods. From high up in the back row at Epidaurus the audience could get a clear view of the performance. The 14,000-seat theater is a huge semicircular bowl cut into the surface of the hillside. Its shape is not just designed for excellent viewing; sound, too is caught and amplified, and actors speaking in the orchestra can be heard in the back row.

Discover Ancient Greece

Aeschylus, the chorus played a central role by commenting in poetic language on the action. Later works increased attention on the dialogue and conflict between individuals, which is still the primary interaction in theatrical productions. Greece's foremost comedic writer was Aristophanes, whose plays were performed at festivals to honor Dionysus, the god of wine.

Ancient Greeks also established the careful practice of writing history, led by historians Herodotus and Thucydides, who recorded wars and other important events in Greece's history.

Greek philosophers had a love of learning and questioned and discussed everything in the universe. They believed that reason and philosophy rather than emotion and rhetoric should rule people's lives. In philosophy and politics, the works of Plato and Aristotle have been among the most influential in Western civilization.

Great Legacy of Arts and Culture

Plato advocated an ideal society that sought beauty and truth. Plato was a student of the great philosopher Socrates, who taught young men in the Athenian marketplace by asking questions and engaging them in dialogues to try to solve difficult problems. Socrates taught that wisdom is knowing that you know nothing. Plato's works try to recapture the style and ideas of his former teacher. He is known for his great work *The Republic*, in which he states that the ideal form of government is one led by philosophers. Plato's own student, Aristotle, later founded a school called the Lyceum, which fostered a scientific appreciation of the natural world.

Science, Mathematics, and Medicine

The ancient Greeks replaced gods with reason to explain the forces in nature. The scientist Archimedes found that the volume

Delphi was considered to be the center of the world in ancient times. It was home to the Pythian games, the forerunner of the Olympic Games, as well as the famed Oracle and Sanctuary of Pythian Apollo.

of an object can be measured by the amount of water it displaces. It is said that he discovered this while taking a bath. Euclid, a mathematician, explained his ideas about geometry in a book titled *Elements*, which is the basis for modern geometry text-books. Hippocrates, known as the "father of western medicine," believed diseases had natural causes that could be treated. Today, doctors take the Hippocratic Oath to practice medicine according to his ideals.

The Olympics

The first Olympic Games were held in ancient Greece as early as 776 B.C.—the basis for the modern Olympics that are still celebrated today. In ancient times, the Olympic games were a religious festival held every fourth summer at Olympia, in honor of Zeus. More than forty thousand people came from all parts of the ancient

Great Legacy of Arts and Culture

This arched entryway leads to the original Olympic stadium.

Discover Ancient Greece

Greek world, traveling hundreds of miles to attend. This was the largest gathering of Greeks in time of peace. Ancient Greeks were serious about sports, and training for the games was intense. Competitors were required to practice for ten months before they were allowed to participate in the games.

    The earliest Olympic competitions were not team events. The sports events were for the individual and included running, the pentathlon (an event that combined five sports), wrestling, boxing, chariot racing, and foot racing with armor. Because they could neither compete nor even watch the Olympics, Greek women staged their own version of the Olympics called the Heraea to honor Hera, the wife of Zeus. The winners of the Olympics and the Heraea were awarded crowned wreaths of olive leaves and earned fame throughout Greece. To win was the highlight of a

Great Legacy of Arts and Culture

John Godina of the United States spins around while making a qualifying throw during the Athens 2004 Olympics men's shot put in Olympia, Greece. The men's and women's shot put was held in the ancient stadium where the original games were played.

person's life. The Olympics celebrated the Greek ideals of the well-rounded individual: a sound, or healthy, body, and a sound mind. The Olympics continued until A.D. 393 and were revived in Athens in 1896, thus carrying an ancient Greek tradition into modern times. In 2004, the summer games returned to Athens for the first time in more than a century, featuring events in twenty-eight different sports.

The Greek poet Pindar wrote several odes in praise of the ancient Olympics. "But if, my heart, you wish to sing of contests," he wrote in 476 B.C., "look no further for any star warmer than the sun, shining by day through the lonely sky, and let us not proclaim any contest greater than Olympia."[1]

Chapter 6

ALEXANDER the GREAT

Discover Ancient Greece

Perhaps no individual soldier in world history was as feared and respected as Alexander the Great, one of the heroes of ancient Greece. By the age of thirty, he had expanded the Greek empire and conquered most of Asia. In one bold campaign after another, Alexander put down uprisings around Greece and occupied surrounding cities. He was especially eager to seek revenge on Persia, which had invaded Greece 150 years earlier.

Alexander was born in 356 B.C., the son of King Philip II of Macedon and his wife, Olympias. Macedon was an ancient kingdom of northern Greece. Philip was himself a fierce soldier, conquering enemy

King Philip of Macedon's silver mines financed the ambitions which led to his domination of the Greek city-states and never-completed preparations for war with Persia.

Alexander the Great

Ancient gold coin with the face of Alexander the Great. He was one of the world's most successful military and political leaders.

Discover Ancient Greece

states and expanding and training the Macedonian Army. His goal was to conquer Greece and all of the Persian Empire.

While still a teenager, Alexander commanded the Macedonian cavalry that helped his father to win a key victory at Chaeronea in 338 B.C., thus conquering Greece. Under Philip's rule, the city-state system of ancient Greece collapsed as the Macedonians established a centralized monarchy that stretched across Greece.

As the son of a king, Alexander also learned important lessons off the battlefield. He grew up under the guidance of the country's greatest teachers, including Aristotle, the famous writer and philosopher. After his father was assassinated in 336 B.C., Alexander ascended to the throne, becoming king of Macedon.

Alexander quickly set his sights on Persia. Alexander's troops engaged in a battle at Granicus, in what is now Syria.

Alexander the Great

Alexander was nearly killed in that battle. After a fierce and deadly cavalry clash, Alexander claimed victory, executing thousands of Persians. He later sent three hundred Persian suits of armor back to the Greek city of Athens with a message reading, "From Alexander, the son of Philip, and the Greeks, except the Spartans."[1] That message showed Alexander's anger at the Spartans, who had refused to join his campaign against Persia.

From Granicus, Alexander moved on to the city of Gordium. There he was shown the famed "Gordian Knot," a complex knot tied by a Greek king. An ancient myth stated that whoever could untie the knot would rule all of Asia. According to legend, Alexander the Great did not untie the knot, but impatiently sliced through it swiftly with his sword. Ever since, the saying "to cut the Gordian knot" means to

Discover Ancient Greece

Alexander solves the problem of the Gordian knot.

Alexander the Great

solve a difficult problem with a single, quick, decisive action.

After conquering Persia, Alexander led his army on a march that would be one of the most memorable in world history, reaching as far as India. But Alexander made many enemies along the way. Some Greeks criticized Alexander for his policies on intermarriage and tolerance toward other races and cultures, such as Asians.

In 323 B.C., Alexander was planning a sea voyage when he became ill and died, at only thirty-three years old. After his death, Alexander's generals argued about how to divide his empire. They divided it into three sections: Macedonia (which included Greece), Babylonia, and Egypt. Eventually, continual warfare weakened Greece.

Alexander the Great is still considered one of the greatest rulers of the ancient world, extending the vast Greek empire to the farthest boundaries of Persia, north to

Greeks and Persians engaged in furious combat, with a mounted Alexander (extreme left) riding down the opposition. This is part of a frieze on the so-called Alexander Sarcophagus found in a royal cemetery.

Russia, east to India, and south to Egypt. At the time of his death, he ruled the largest empire the world had ever seen. He has remained a lasting symbol of ancient Greece—whose widespread influence in the arts, architecture, and politics can still be seen today.

Alexander and the Hellenistic Period

When Alexander came to power, he successfully expanded Greek civilization and culture across much of Asia and India. Yet, in doing so, Alexander also introduced new cultures to Greek society, changing it forever. Under his reign, Greek city-states became members of a "cosmopolis"—a world of city-states that were no longer self-contained political units.

Alexander's death in 323 B.C. ushered in the Hellenistic Age of ancient Greece in which people from other nations embraced

Alexander the Great

Discover Ancient Greece

Greek intellectual ideas and its artistic contributions. Although this period could be seen as a flowering of Greek culture, it was also marked by increasing internal disorganization and fighting among those who were Alexander's successors.

Seizing the advantage, the Romans were able to conquer much of the ancient Greek Empire. By 146 B.C. the Romans were in control of Greece. Although the rise of the Roman Empire ended Greece's long reign as a political and cultural power, the influence of ancient Greece would continue to be felt around the world for many centuries to come.

TIMELINE

1250–1184 B.C. The war that will provide the basis for the legendary Trojan War is probably fought.

800 B.C. Greeks develop an alphabet and build early temples.

700–500 B.C. Archaic Age in ancient Greece.

760 B.C. First Olympic Games are held.

750–700 B.C. City-state political system emerges; *The Illiad* and *The Odyssey* are written; period of lyric poetry begins.

550 B.C. Sparta becomes dominant on the Peloponnese.

507 B.C. Cleisthenes reforms Athenian constitution; democracy develops.

550–449 B.C. Persian Wars: Battles of Marathon, Thermopylae, Salamis, and Platea; Athens emerges as most powerful city-state in Greece.

490 B.C. Beginning of the classical Age and style in art and sculpture.

461–431 B.C. Golden Age of Athens under the leadership of Pericles.

447–432 B.C. The Parthenon is constructed in Athens and Sparta are fought.

Discover Ancient Greece

431–404 B.C. Peloponnesian Wars between Athens and Sparta are fought.

404–377 B.C. Sparta rules as the powerful city-state in Greece

347 B.C. Plato founds the Academy.

342 B.C. Aristotle begins teaching Alexander, son of King Philip of Macedon.

338 B.C. Philip of Macedon defeats Athens at battle of Chaerones; conquers Greece.

336 B.C. Alexander succeeds his father Philip upon his death.

334–333 B.C. Alexander defeats Perisians at battles of Grancius and Issus; cuts the Gordian Knot.

332 B.C. Alexander conquers Egypt.

327–325 B.C. Alexander invades Northern India.

323 B.C. Alexander dies; his generals vie for power.

323–143 B.C. The Hellenistic Age marks shift toward multiethnic population and culture.

GLOSSARY

acropolis—A Greek fort built high on a hill.

agora—An marketplace or public space.

A.D.—The letters stand for Anno Domini, meaning "in the the Year of our Lord" and are placed before the date starting with A.D. 1.

assembly—Gathering of people and officials that control life.

B.C.— The letters stand for "Before Christ" and are placed after the date 1 B.C.

city-state—A city that is like an independent country.

civilization—A kind of culture marked by a high level of organization in government and religion. Trade, writing, and art are all a part of civilization.

column—A slender upright structure used in architecture to support a roof, an upper story, or the top part of a wall.

council—Five-hundred person legislative body that arranged the business of the assembly.

constitution—A plan for government; a document stating the basic laws and principles of a government.

Corinthian—one of the three principle styles in classical architecture. Corinthian columns have

Discover Ancient Greece

elaborate bell-shaped capitals decorated with carved stone leaves.

democracy—A government in which citizens rule and share power.

Doric—one of the three principle styles in classical architecture. Doric columns are solid with wide fluting and a plain, round top.

empire—A nation and the country it rules.

Ionic—one of the three principle styles in classical architecture. Ionic columns are are slender with narrow fluting, and a scrolled capital.

isthmus—A narrow strip of land that connects two larger pieces of land.

lyre—A musical instrument with strings that is like a harp.

oracle—Sacred place where ancient Greeks could ask their gods, through a priestess, to give them advice or to foretell the future.

ostrakon—A fragment of stone or pottery inscribed with writing or drawing.

peninsula—A narrow strip of land extending out to the sea that is almost completely surrounded by water.

philosophy—The study of wisdom and truth.

polis—The Greek word for city-state.

slave—A man, woman, or child who is owned by another person in the same way as a piece of property, usually to do work of some kind.

CHAPTER NOTES

Chapter 1. THE LAND AND EARLY HISTORY
1. Thucydides, The History of the Peloponnesian War, Book 1, Chapter 12, "The Internet Classic Archive," n.d., <http://classics.mit.edu/Thucydides/pelopwar.html> (April 27, 2004).

Chapter 2. LIFE OF THE PEOPLE
1. Sarah B. Pomeroy, et. al. Ancient Greece: A Political, Social, and Cultural History (New York: Oxford University Press, 1999), p. 235.

Chapter 3. ANCIENT GREEK GOVERNMENT
1. Sarah B. Pomeroy, et. al. Ancient Greece: A Political, Social, and Cultural History (New York: Oxford University Press, 1999), p. 355.

Chapter 4. THE CITY-STATE AND WARS
1. Jacob Burckhardt, The Greeks and Greek Civilization (New York: St. Martin's Press, 1998), p. 293.

Chapter 5. GREAT LEGACY OF ARTS AND CULTURE
1. Pindar, translation by Diane Svarlien, Odes (1990), available from the Perseus Project, n.d., <www.perseus.tufts.edu> (December 7, 2003).

Chapter 6. ALEXANDER THE GREAT
1. Sarah B. Pomeroy, et. al. Ancient Greece: A Political, Social, and Cultural History (New York: Oxford University Press, 1999), p. 403.

FURTHER READING

BOOKS

Gay, Kathlyn. *Science in Ancient Greece*. London, U.K.: Franklin Watts, 1998.

Hull, Robert. *Ancient Greece*. New York: Gareth Stevens, 2011.

Kerrigan, Michael. *Greeks*. New York: Benchmark Books, 2010.

Napoli, Donna Jo. *Treasury of Greek Mythology: Classic Stories of Gods, Goddesses, Heroes & Monsters*. Washington, D.C.: National Geographic Children's Books, 2011.

Pearson, Anne. *Ancient Greece*. New York: DK Publishing, 2007

Powell, Anton. *Ancient Greece*. New York: Chelsea House, 2007.

Steele, Philip. *Ancient Greece*. Boston, MA: Kingfisher, 2011

Villing, Alexandra. *The Ancient Greeks: Their Lives and Their World*. Los Angeles: J. Paul Getty Museum, 2010.

INTERNET ADDRESSES

Ancient Greece—The British Museum
<www.ancientgreece.co.uk>

BBC—Primary History—Ancient Greece
<www.bbc.co.uk/schools/primaryhistory/ancient_greeks/>

INDEX

A
Aeschylus, 72–76
Alexander the Great, 86–96
Amphipolis, battle at, 63
Aphrodite, 37–38
Apollo, 38
Archaic Age of Greece, 52–54
Ares, 38
Argos, 54
Aristophanes, 76
Aristotle, 76–77, 88
Athena, 37, 60, 70–72
Athens, 8, 23, 29, 33, 43–44, 48–50, 56–63, 65–71, 84, 89

B
Babylonia, 91
Bronze Age Greece, 12

C
city-states, rise of, 22–23
Cleisthenes, 44
Corinth, 9, 54
Crete, 9–13

D
Darius I, 54–56
Dark Age of Greece, 16–21
Delian League, 58, 62
Delphi, 38
Dionysus, 76

E
education, 33–34
Egypt, 23, 36, 54, 91–94
Euclid, 80
Euripides, 48–72

G
geography and climate, 8–12, 28
Golden Age of Greece, 65
government, 22–23, 25, 41–50, 52, 68, 77, 88
Granicus, battle at, 88–89

H
Hellenistic Age, 94–96
Hera, 38, 82
Heracles, 17, 39
Heraea, 82
Herodotus, 76

Discover Ancient Greece

Hippocrates, 80
Homer, 16, 33, 36, 72

I
Iliad, The, 16, 72
Ionia, 20
Isocrates, 63

L
Leonidas, 57
Lysander, 63

M
Macedon, kingdom of, 86–88
Marathon, battle at, 56
Minoan civilization, 12–13
Mycenaean civilization, 13–17
mythology and religion, 13, 16, 36–39

O
Odyssey, The, 16, 72
Olympia, 38, 80, 84
Olympic Games, 65, 80–84
Olympus, Mount, 8, 36

P
Parthenon, 71–72
Peloponnese, 9, 13, 23, 54
Peloponnesian League, 62
Peloponnesian War, 43, 62–62, 65
Pericles, 63, 65–71

Persephone, 37, 39
Persian Empire, 54–60
Persian Wars, 54–60, 65
Philip II, 86–89
Pindar, 84
Plataea, battle at, 58
Plato, 76–77
Poseidon, 37, 72

R
Republic, The, 77
Rhodes, 9
Roman Empire, 96

S
Salamis, battle at, 58
Sappho, 72
Socrates, 77
Sophocles, 72
Sparta, 9, 16, 23, 33–34, 43, 49–50, 54, 57–63, 65, 89

T
Themistocles, 58
Thermopylae, battle at, 57–58
Thucydides, 17, 76
Trojan War, 15–16
Troy, 15–17

X
Xerxes I, 56–57, 60

Z
Zeus, 37–39, 80–82